Golf Slow Motion Picture Swing Secrets Of Effortless Long Shots

Accu-Golf Systems

Outskirts Press, Inc
Denver, Colorado

Golf Slow Motion Picture Swing Secrets of Effortless Long Shots
All Rights Reserved
Copyright © 2006 Richard Chen
Cover Art Courtesy of Hemera Technologies

Outskirts Press
http://www.outskirtspress.com

ISBN-10: 1-59800-400-X
ISBN-13: 978-1-59800-400-7

Outskirts Press and the "OP" logo are trademarks belonging to
Outskirts Press, Inc.

Printed in the United States of America

Table of Contents

Introduction

Golf Slow Motion Picture Swing Secrets of Effortless Long Shots

The secrets of great golf swings are undeniably captured in the many slow-motion-picture sequences of champions. The secrets are there for all to see. Yet, like hieroglyphics, it is difficult to understand what the pictures are telling us. Pictures contain a myriad of information. The secret is to be able to understand the key information in the pictures.

This book presents information on how to see the key golf-swing motions used by champions to hit great and long golf shots.

Slow-motion-picture sequences of the swings of champions are available everywhere in golf magazines, golf books, and now on Internet Web sites. There are literally hundreds of these slow-motion golf swing picture sequences of championship-level golfers available. The problem is to understand, and to be able to see the key motions that all of these super golfers use to consistently hit great shots—golf shots that are long and true. Valuable information is contained in these picture sequences, but to be able to see the "secrets" is another matter. It is necessary to know the secrets before hand in order to recognize the secrets in the pictures. This book points out exactly where in the pictures to look for answers to the most important golf-swing secrets—golf secrets such as what the champions do to swing the clubhead from the inside to the outside to draw the ball, to consistently hit the ball off the fairway, and to hit the ball long and straight.

The ultimate secret of golf may be the phenomenon of hitting long shots with seemingly "effortless" swings.   All golfers have occasionally produced very long shots with seemingly effortless swings. It is a great mystery to them how they accomplish this.   If only they could understand this mystery, they could reproduce these long and effortless shots with regularity. This book presents, for the first time, a clear and simple explanation of how long shots can be produced from seemingly effortless swings.   In explaining how long shots can be produced seemingly effortlessly, this book may perhaps be the most significant golf book published in recent times, if not for all times.

With the clear, and to the point, explanations presented in this book, readers can see for themselves from the slow-motion pictures what secrets are used by the champions to produce great golf shots that fly long and true.

CHAPTER 1

The Efficient Inside-to-Outside Downswing

Slow-motion-picture sequences show that all champions perform the Inside-to-Outside Swing. This is the primary difference separating the great golfers from the poor golfers: the Inside-to-Outside Swing.

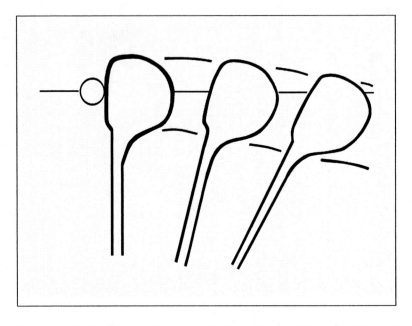

Figure 1-1. Inside to Outside Swing Path of the Clubhead

The champions swing the clubhead from the inside to the outside, while the poor golfers do the opposite and swing the clubhead from the outside to the inside. In other words, the poor golfer swings the clubhead on a path that imparts a "cut spin" or "slice spin" to the ball.

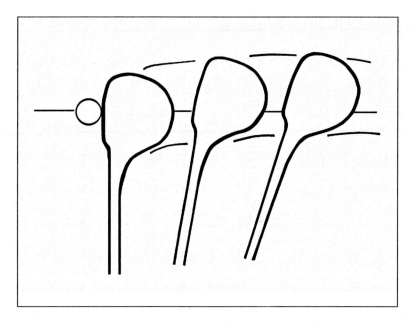

Figure 1-2. Outside to Inside Swing Path of the Clubhead

The standard and common golfing terminology such as *inside*, *outside*, *clubhead swing path*, and *slice* may not be familiar to many who have not been exposed to golfing literature. These terms and concepts are explained in detail, and with many diagrams, in the appendices in the back of this book. By placing these details in the back of the book, the main points of the swings of champions will not be diminished by these details. Appendix A describes the slice. Appendix B describes the inside and outside areas as well as the many possible clubhead swing paths.

As in Ping-Pong, or in tennis, a cut or slice spin significantly reduces the distance the ball travels. This can be used to advantage in Ping-Pong and tennis to shorten the shot and to make the ball curve and bounce to the right to surprise the opponent. For a normal golf shot, however, the slice spin greatly reduces the distance of the golf shot and causes the golf ball to curve drastically to the right. Both of these effects result in poor golf. The reduced distance makes reaching greens in regulation golf extremely difficult. The slice curving to the right puts the ball into the trees lining the right side of the fairway. A cut or slice spin is used in tennis to purposely shorten the shot, and to make the ball bounce to the right. It works the same way in golf. It is not the normal shot.

The normal swings of champions are structured to prevent the slice spin. This is the first thing to look for in the slow-motion-picture sequences of champions. What are the motions used by all champions to swing the clubhead from the Inside-to-Outside instead of from the Outside-to-Inside?

It is not easy or natural to swing the clubhead from the inside to the outside; otherwise, golf would be an easy game. Golf is difficult because it is unnatural to swing the clubhead on an Inside-to-Outside swing path. Most champions start playing golf at a very young age. Some have even started playing when they were babies. This early playing allows the unnatural Inside-to-Outside swing to become more natural. Even so, top golfers still need to practice constantly to perform this Inside-to-Outside swing well.

The most important picture to analyze is that of the first phase of the downswing. It is the first phase of the downswing that decides whether the clubhead will be swung correctly from the inside, or not.

It is common sense that to start the clubhead traveling from the inside, it is necessary to keep the clubhead as far inside as reasonable during the start of the downswing. The stop-action picture shows how Tiger Woods, or any other champion accomplishes this during the first part of the downswing:

- Right shoulder is still to the rear, until the release
- The hands tilt the club shaft back to the rear of the golfer
- The upper body is closed, and it faces somewhat away from the target
- The left arm is about parallel with the target line just before the release

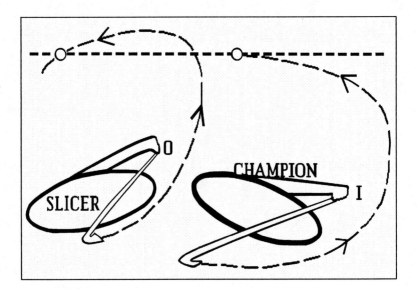

Figure 1-3. Hand and Arm Positions of Slicer and Champion

The above picture illustrates the key differences between the champion and the slicer just before the start of the release midway in the downswing. The champion's hands are at Point I, which is further inside than the hands of the slicer at Point O. The right shoulder of the champion is farther to the rear than the slicer's. The chest of the champion is facing away from the target, while the chest of the slicer is facing toward the target. The left arm of the champion is about parallel with the target line, while the left arm of the slicer has swung out toward the target line. As a result, the clubhead in the champion's swing remains inside of the target line until impact. However, the clubhead of the slicer swings outside of the target line, and then it has to be pulled back to the target line to hit the ball. A cut shot results in putting a slice spin on the slicer's ball.

With the clubhead kept well inside during the initial downswing phase, a great swing is in the making. It takes two points to determine a line. The next picture shows the end point for the hands for the initial phase of the downswing. This point is a magical point in the downswing. It is the point when the hands start to release. It is also the same point for the hands at the right-most end of the waggle during setup. This point will be labeled as "R" in the picture. Point R is a magical point in the downswing when the hands start to release by uncocking the wrists.

The key observations at the start of hand release for the champions are:

- The shoulders are still slightly closed and coiled.
- The hands are relatively close to the body.
- The back of the left hand faces to the front of the golfer in a karate-chop orientation.
- The hands are still inside at Point R.

Figure 1-4. Hand Position at the Start of the Release

The above picture from a slow-motion sequence of Jack Nicklaus shows the start of the release phase of the downswing. These positions encourage an Inside-to-Outside swing path for the clubhead. Even though Nicklaus plays a fade with the feet set in an open position with the left foot slightly more to the rear than the right foot, his swing is still based on the Inside-to-Outside swing. His right shoulder is still more to the rear than the left shoulder. The chest faces slightly away from the target even though the hip is facing somewhat toward the target at this point. The head is tilted slightly away from the direction of the target. The hips are less open than those of Woods, who is more flexible. Champions are more flexible than average. They swing with relaxed waist muscles to allow the chest to face away from the target, while the hips turn toward the target.

If the hands swing down to a point that is farther out from the player than Point R, the hands will be too far outside, and the clubhead will push to an Outside-to-Inside swing path. A slice results.

Point R truly is a magical point for the left hand to swing through. For when the hands swing through Point R during the initial release phase of the downswing, the hands will swing the clubhead on an inside path. This almost ensures that the clubhead will travel along the Inside-to-Outside, or the Inside-to-Outside-to-Straight clubhead swing paths. The ball will be hit with maximum efficiency because no slice spin will be imparted to the ball.

The ball will also be hit harder because the shoulders are more fully coiled at the start of the release when the hands are at position R rather than at position O. From the picture above, the champion has the right shoulder farther back, and he has the left shoulder farther away from the target.

The shoulders of the champion are more coiled at the start of the release. By retaining more of the shoulder coil going into the release, the champion is able to provide more shoulder unwinding during the release. This retention of shoulder coil increases the power of the shoulder turn during the release phase of the downswing to generate significantly more clubhead speed to hit the ball longer.

When the hands swing through Point R, they swing relatively close to the body. This relative closeness of the hands to the body can be seen by noticing that the right elbow tucks into the right side of the body. This tucking of the right elbow into the right side of the body occurs automatically when the hands swing through Point R. When the hands swing through point R, the right elbow tucks into the right side of the body.

Slow-motion-picture sequences show many champions tuck their right elbows into the right sides of their bodies during the initial phase of the downswing. This means that they all are swinging their hands through Point I and then through Point R. This also means that the club shaft will swing closer to the body during the downswing. By swinging the club shaft closer to the body, the club handle is more under the right hand than if the club shaft is swung far away from the body. With the club handle more under the right hand, the right hand can more easily press down to provide more power to the shot. Besides being a magical point for creating the proper Inside-to-Outside swing path, Point R provides more power to the shot.

Examining the different slow-motion-picture sequences of different champions will show all of these champions swinging their hands close to Point R rather than through Point O. This similarity shows that all champions swing the clubhead along the Inside-to-Outside path. In addition, all of these pictures show that at the start of the release, the champions have their shoulders somewhat closed. That is, their right shoulders are still further to the back than their left shoulders at the start of the release phase of the downswing. In another words, their shoulders still retain a fair amount of coil at the start of the release to power the release. All of the champions use these swing positions to swing the clubhead on the proper inside path and to generate clubhead speed. No slow-motion pictures of normal shots of champions will ever show them swinging their hands through the outside Point O, and none of these pictures will ever show their shoulders not to be somewhat closed and coiled at the start of the release.

These pictures give evidence that the champions all swing their hands through Point I and then through Point R during the downswing. It is the magical Point R that almost automatically creates championship-quality golf shots. Pictures of Tiger Woods swinging through Point I during the initial phase of the downswing are shown below:

Figure 1-5. Top View at Midpoint of the Downswing

The above stop-action picture shows the top view of Tiger Woods swinging through Point I during the initial phase of the downswing. The left arm has swung down to approximately a horizontal position. The left arm is about parallel with the target line. The shoulders are still pointing somewhat away from the target in a somewhat closed position even though his hips are very open. The right shoulder is still behind the head.

The head is turned slightly away from the direction of the target. Thus, the clubhead is kept well to the inside. The clubhead swing path is set for the ideal Inside-to-Outside swing path.

Slow-motion-picture sequences show that all champions swing through Point I and then through Point R. Thereby, they keep the clubhead to the inside during the initial phase of the downswing. However, there are significant variations between the swings of different champions, as shown by their different picture sequences. The different body builds of the champions dictate variations in their swings. No two champions are built exactly alike. They swing differently according to their different builds. They swing naturally. While many champions draw the ball, where the ball takes on a trajectory that curves from right to left, many other champions do the opposite and fade the ball. The fade is a small version of the slice, where the ball curves from left to right, but not to a great extend. There is no one swing that will fit all.

Unlike the champions, the poor golfers have their hands full just worrying about making contact with the ball. They are also too preoccupied with generating clubhead speed. The poor golfers don't spend time worrying about the clubhead swing path. The champions know that both the clubhead swing path and making contact with the ball are important. As a matter of fact, clubhead swing path is more important than making good contact with the ball. It is like landing a plane. The approach is more important than the touch down. If the approach is bad, a good touch down is almost impossible, and a disaster follows.

CHAPTER 2

The Powerful Release

The release phase of the downswing is generally described as the uncocking of the wrists to hit the ball. The release, however, is a lot more than that. The primary functions of the release are:

- To swing the clubhead along the final Inside-to-Outside (and then to Straight) path into the ball
- To close the clubface from open to square at impact
- To position the hands at the proper position over the ball at impact
- To accelerate the clubhead to maximum speed

A. Final Inside-to-Outside Path

Slow-motion-picture sequences at Point R show that the back of the left hand faces out away from the front of the golfer rather than toward the target. The left hand takes a karate-chop orientation. The left thumb points in the opposite direction from the target. From these orientations of the hands and the left forearm, the clubhead is kept to the inside at the start of the release.

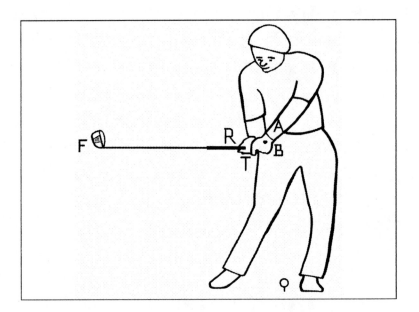

Figure 2-1. Upper Body Positions Early in the Release

In the above slow-motion picture, the back of the left hand at Point B is facing out at about right angles to the target line. The left forearm at Point A is also facing out away from the golfer. The left thumb at Point T is pointing in an opposite direction from the target. It is pointing toward Point F in the picture. The hands are kept relatively close to the right side of the body at Point R. The shoulders are slightly closed facing slightly away from the target. The net result is that the clubhead is kept well inside, at Point F, at the start of the release.

As the release progresses, the shoulders begin to rotate from a somewhat closed position to a slightly opened position. In another words, the chest starts to face a little toward the target. The arms swing farther downward and slightly outward as the natural result of the arms' swinging and the shoulders' rotating. The left hand and the left forearm start to rotate counterclockwise. The left thumb begins to point down and toward the ball. In the case of the driver, the right hand palm starts to face less skyward and less open. These actions start to swing the clubhead down and out toward the ball. They also begin to square the clubface. Notice that in the below picture, the clubhead is between the Target Line and the feet. The clubhead is still in the Inside Area halfway into the release.

Figure 2-2. Midway Point of the Release

B. Closing the Clubface from Open to Square

The clubface at Point F at the early part of the release is wide open. The clubface is pointing approximately at a right angle to the target line instead of at the target. The wide-open clubface at the start of release is the result of keeping the clubhead well inside at Point F.

The two opposing choices are to have the clubface closing early before impact but to have the clubhead less inside early in the release, or having the clubface wide open to keep the clubhead more to the inside. It should be obvious by now that the primary choice of the champions is to keep the clubhead on the inside path. Having the clubface closing early is sacrificed to gaining a better inside path. In most slow-motion-picture sequences of the champions, the clubface is not squared until just before impact. This late squaring of the clubface promotes a more certain Inside-to-Outside swing path, but a less certain clubface angle at impact. As a result, champions consistently hit long shots promoted by the Inside-to-Outside swing path, while they are less consistent in the directions of the shots as a result of squaring the clubface late in the release.

There is a special move advocated by Ben Hogan to start squaring the clubface early and still maintain a good Inside-to-Outside swing path for the clubhead during the release. It is like having one's cake and eating it too. Hogan points out that many fine players of his era pronate the left wrist during the release. The left hand is bend back slightly with the top of the left wrist forming a slight hump. This allows the left hand and the left forearm to rotate counterclockwise early in the release to close the clubface while still keeping the clubhead well inside during the release. However, most modern champions do not make this complex move. This wrist orientation is brought up as some slow-motion-picture sequences of some champions of the past show this wrist orientation.

The clubface points in the same general direction as the back of the left hand, the top of the left forearm, the palm of the right hand, and the inside of the right forearm. At the start of the release, they face about 90 degrees away from the target. For the long clubs, they are also tilting slightly skyward, which further keeps the clubhead inside. By the time of impact, they face toward the target. At the start of the release, the shoulders are somewhat closed. At impact, the shoulders are somewhat open. For the driver, the palm of the right hand is open and faces slightly upward to the sky at the start of the release. The right palm then turns toward the target just before impact. The left thumb points horizontally away from the target at the start of the release. At impact, the left thumb points down in the general direction of the ball. Thus, the clubface is squared at impact, with the clubhead traveling on an Inside-to-Outside path into the ball. A great shot is in the making.

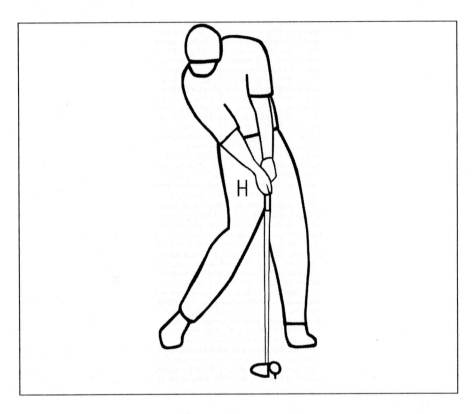

Figure 2-3. Impact

Although the left thumb is obscured by the right hand in the slow-motion-picture sequences, the direction to which the left thumb points can be inferred from the picture sequences. The left thumb points away from the target at the start of the release. It points down in the general direction of the ball at impact. It then points in the direction of the target early in the follow-through.

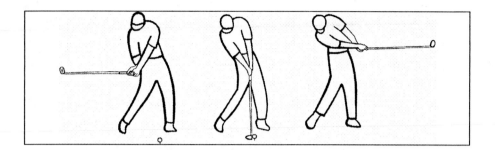

Figure 2-4. Left Thumb Directions of the Release

C. Position of the Hands at Impact

Slow-motion pictures of the champions show that the hands are about even with the ball at impact for the teed-up driver. For all other shots, excepting the putter perhaps, the hands are in front of the ball at impact. The phrase "hands are in front of the ball" means that the hands are closer to the target than the ball is. In the stop-action frontal picture of a right-handed golfer, the hands are closer to the right edge of the picture than the ball is. The position of the hands at impact is so important and basic to the golf shot that it will be more fully treated in the next chapter.

D. Accelerating the Clubhead to Maximum Speed

Slow-motion-picture sequences and stroboscopic picture sequences show that about half or more of the total clubhead speed is generated during the release. Whether the hands are consciously used during the release to accelerate the club seems to depend on the individual styles of the champions. Some consciously apply the hands during release, while others do not consciously apply the hands during the release. Some of this may depend on the strength of their hands. Hogan said that he applied the right hand strongly during the release. Nicklaus on the other hand said that he did not consciously apply the hands at all during the release. Some of this may depend on the length of the club shaft. With extra-long shafts, the clubhead travels on a longer path, giving more time to consciously use the hands. With the short clubs, there is little time to consciously use the hands as the clubhead travels on a shorter path.

Nicklaus popularized the no-waggle golf swing, as he does not waggle the club before taking the backswing. On the other end of the spectrum, Hogan had specified the waggle as one of the five fundamentals of the golf swing. He advocated daily practicing of the waggle and the release in the form of back and forth slow miniature swings. The waggle can promote hitting the ball on the sweet spot. More importantly, the waggle can be used to groove the proper Inside-to-Outside path during the release. It is a dress rehearsal of the critical release phase of the downswing. However, the waggle normally does not promote a rehearsal of high clubhead acceleration. By necessity, the waggle has to be relatively slow; otherwise, the clubhead cannot be stopped before contacting the ball during the waggle. As a result, the hand and forearm muscles are overly relaxed instead of working enough during the waggle. This excessive relaxation increases the chance of a weak release during the actual downswing. Slow-motion-picture sequences show the champions make full releases. At the start of the release, the back of the left hand faces forward, and soon after impact, the back of the left hand faces inward. At the start of the release, the right palm faces outward, and it faces inward soon after impact. Additionally, in the case of the driver, the palm of the right hand faces slightly skyward during the early part of the release besides it being open, and it faces slightly downward besides inward soon after impact. At the start of the release, the left thumb points away from the target. Soon after impact, the left thumb points toward the target. These picture sequences show that the champions make full and forceful releases.

Ultra-slow-motion-picture sequences have been made to show how the ball is compressed by the clubface during impact. The back of the ball is compressed for a few sixteenths of an inch during the impact. If the waggle is performed with the thought of compressing the back of the ball without actually contacting the ball, of course, the muscles can be trained to provide necessary force during the release.

On the whole, it can be said that the release is where the champions provide maximum acceleration to the clubhead, and not before. This is common sense as seen in the slow-motion-picture sequences. It is during the release that the clubhead finally starts to travel on a path that closely matches the target line. Before the release, the clubhead is still traveling downward in the direction of the ground. Any premature drastic acceleration of the clubhead will cause the clubhead to dig into the ground before it is able to contact the ball.

While golfers, and even champions, expend a lot of effort in trying to gain distance, there is a phenomenon in golf of the very long shot produced by an effortless swing. The extra long shots are produced by seemingly "easy" swings. Even poor golfers who normally do not hit the ball very far have occasionally hit very long shots with seemingly effortless and seemingly easy swings. It is just that they rarely produce such shots. Such long and effortless shots are rare accidents for them. The search for the secret of the long and effortless swing is one of the grails of golf. In a later chapter on distance, detailed explanations are presented for the first time on how relatively modest amount of energy is required to produce the long ones. Using extremely simple and scientifically derived formulas, that chapter shows the reason why seemingly effortless and easy swings can produce the long ones. Once explained by these simple and natural formulas, the "effortless" swing can be repeatedly generated at will to consistently produce an endless number of long ones. These formulas explain why the champions consistently hit long ones, even though they are not always so consistent in direction.

CHAPTER 3

Consistent Impact

The position of the champions at the point of impact is the next most important aspect to analyze in the slow-motion-picture sequences. The impact is when the clubhead contacts the ball. There are many things to look for in the picture of the impact, but the key aspect is the position of the hands at the moment of impact. While a lot of movements of every part of the body, including the uncocking of the hands, occur between Point I and Point H, the position of the hands at Point H has extreme significance, especially for fairway shots. The slow-motion pictures of the champions show that the hands are in front of the ball at the moment the clubhead contacts the ball for all non-teed-up shots. That is, for all fairway shots, the hands lead the clubhead into the ball. The hands are closer to the target than the ball at the moment the clubhead hits the ball, which is sitting on the turf. In the case of a teed-up ball hit with a driver, the hands are approximately even with the ball at the moment of contact. Thus, there are two H points: one for the teed-up driver shot and one for all non-teed-up shots. The key observations are:

- Hands are about even with the ball at the moment of impact for the teed-up drive

- Hands are in front of the ball at the moment of impact for all other shots

The stop-action picture shows the following key observations when the hands have swung down to the impact point:

- For hitting non-teed-up shots off of the fairway, the hands are slightly closer to the target than the ball at the moment the clubhead contacts the ball. In other words, the hands are in front, or ahead, of the ball at the moment of impact.

- For hitting teed-up shots with a driver, the hands are approximately even with the ball at the moment of impact.

A. Hands in Front of the Ball for Fairway Shots

Slow-motion-picture sequences of non-teed-up shots show that the champions have the hands ahead of the ball at the moment of impact. In other words, the top of the club handle at Point H is ahead of the ball at Point C at the moment the clubhead contacts the ball. This means that the clubhead has hit the ball while the clubhead is still traveling on the downward part of the swing arc.

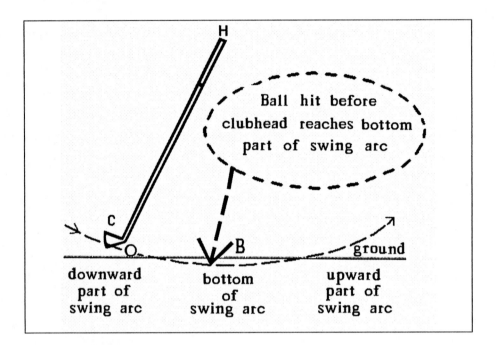

Figure 3-1. Top of Club Ahead of Ball at Impact for Fairway Shots

Slow-motion-picture sequences of champions hitting irons and fairway woods off the fairway show that the hands and the top of the club are decidedly in front of the clubhead and the ball at the moment of impact. In the above diagram, the top of the club at Point H is closer to the right edge of the diagram than the clubhead at Point C when the ball is contacted. This means that the ball is hit while the clubhead is still traveling on the downward part of the swing arc. This provides a clean contact of the clubface with the ball before the clubhead digs into the ground at the bottom of the swing at Point B.

If the hands are behind the ball at impact instead of being in front of the ball, it means that the ball is to be hit on the upward arc of the swing. The chances are that the clubhead will dig into the ground before the ball is contacted.

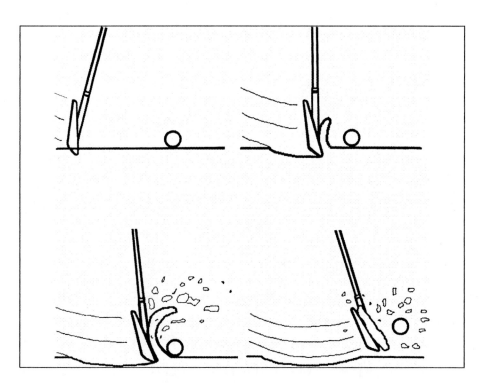

Figure 3-2. Fat Shot When Hands Behind the Ball at Impact for Fairway Shots

When the ball is hit on the upswing with the hands behind the ball at impact, the clubhead has already dipped down into the ground before contacting the ball. A slice of divot has been dug up, which is interposed between the clubface and the ball. The shot is softened tremendously by the interposing divot, and all distance of the shot is lost.

B. Hands Even with the Ball for the Drive

Slow-motion-picture sequences show that the hands are approximately even with the ball at the moment of impact for the teed-up drive. If the hands are too far in front of or too far behind the ball, the clubface will be left either too open or too closed at the moment of impact. For the drive, most modern champions advocate hitting the ball at the exact bottom of the swing arc. This would imply that the top of the club handle should line up with the back of the ball at the exact moment of impact. However, slow-motion pictures do show some slight variations.

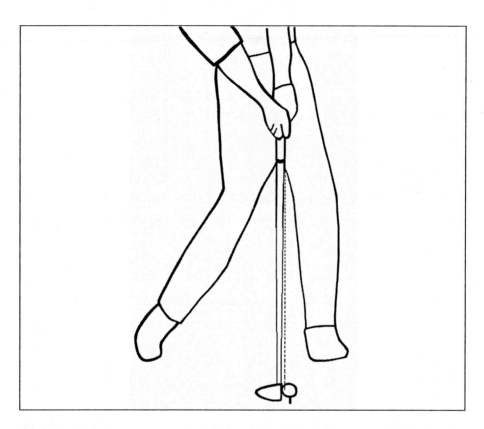

Figure 3-3. Hand and Top of Club Even with the Back of the Ball

Starting with the wedge and short irons, slow-motion-picture sequences show the hands are significantly in front of the ball at the moment of impact. With the long irons and fairway woods, the hands are less, but still noticeably, in front of the ball at the moment of impact. This hand lead allows the ball to be hit on the downward part of the clubhead swing arc. The clubface will thus contact the ball before contacting the ground. Clean hits will result.

Hand lead does reduce the clubface loft slightly. However, the irons and even the shorter fairway woods have enough clubface loft so that there is still plenty of loft remaining. A clean contact imparts the most backspin to the ball. It is backspin that keeps the ball flying for the maximum distance.

Hand lead also opens the clubface slightly. As a result, the clubface has to be hooded slightly to keep the clubface square. The hooding reduces the clubface loft somewhat. For irons, this reduction is not a problem as even long irons have fair amounts of clubface loft. For the driver with little clubface loft, the reduction of loft can become a problem. To avoid the clubface loft reduction from hooding, or to avoid leaving the clubface slightly open, the driver is hit with essentially no hand lead.

Obviously, the amount of hand lead

depends on the individual champion's style of playing and on the equipment used. What the slow-motion-picture sequences do show is the consistency of the hand positions at the moment of impact. Consistency of hand positions at impact enables the champions to consistently hit the ball cleanly off of the fairways for great distances, and to gain directional accuracy.

CHAPTER 4

Secret Distance Formulas of the Effortless Swing

S low-motion-picture sequences and stroboscopic pictures of champion golfers show the steady acceleration of the clubhead to generate clubhead speed. The clubhead accelerates steadily during the initial part of the downswing as the natural result of the shoulders' unwinding. The maximum acceleration is applied during the release as the arms swing and the wrists' uncocking.

A. Introduction to the Distance Formulas

As described in the previous chapters, clubhead speed by itself does not result in maximum distance, unless the clubhead speed is applied in the most efficient manner. In other words, unless clubhead speed is applied in the Inside-to-Outside (and then to Straight) direction to hit the ball, less than maximum distance will result. That is why all champion golfers swing Inside-to-Outside, or they swing Inside-to-Outside-to-Straight, to gain maximum efficiency.

If, instead, an Outside-to-Inside cut swing is used, efficiency will be drastically decreased. This Outside-to-Inside slice swing will make the ball fly higher and more to the right instead of forward toward the target. The harder the ball is hit with a slice swing, the higher the ball will fly and the more it will curve to the right. Almost all of the extra energy will be wasted in making the ball go higher and to the right. It is almost like hitting the ball to a brick wall that prevents the ball from going forward.

Thus, it is seen from the pictures that champions swing the clubhead within the Inside Area for as long as possible during the downswing just before the ball is hit, even at the sacrifice of some clubhead speed. They keep the shoulders closed for most of the downswing until the final release. Their chests face away from the target for most of the downswing until the final part of the release. The back of the left hand and the palm of the right hand are kept opened almost until impact. Many of them actually set up with the heads turned somewhat away from the target to ease their ability to keep their shoulders turned away from the target for most of the initial part of the downswing.

Since the Inside Area is rather narrow and confining as compared to the Outside Area, the pro swings look rather restricted. The shoulders unwind modestly during the initial part of the downswing with the right shoulder appearing to dip down more than turn. Contrary to swinging a baseball bat, throwing a ball, or throwing a punch, the pro's golf swing is not a roundhouse swing.

Even though the pro's downswing appears straitjacketed, it is efficient. All of the clubhead speed generated in an Inside-to-Outside swing is translated into forward ball distance. Most of the clubhead speed generated in the inefficient Outside-to-Inside swing is wasted in diverting the ball high and far to the right.

Besides knowing that the Inside-to-Outside and the Inside-to-Outside-to-Straight swings are very efficient in moving the ball forward, it is necessary to understand some simple physics of propelling the ball forward with clubhead speed. How much clubhead speed is needed to create long shots? The answer is surprisingly modest as will be explained in the remainder of the chapter. It may seem that a great deal of clubhead speed is necessary to hit those long ones. This is a misconception created by the slice shot. As mentioned before, the slice shot is so inefficient that a tremendous amount of energy is needed to hit the long ones, as most of the energy is wasted. The more energy is applied in a slice swing, the more inefficient the slice shot becomes as it moves less forward and moves higher and farther to the right. The slicer swings wildly all out in the hope of gaining more distance, but not much distance is actually gained, if at all. It seems that a tremendous amount of energy is needed to gain a few extra yards, or even a single yard. Often it seems that the harder a slicer swings, the shorter the ball goes. This is because the ball starts to curve drastically to the right. Sometimes the ball can curve almost at right angles to the right. Shorter distance also results as all-out wild swings cause the ball to be hit farther away from the sweet spot of the clubface, resulting in weak shots and further distance losing.

Assuming the ball is hit with an efficient Inside-to-Outside swing, and with the ball hit on the sweet spot of the clubface, relatively modest amount of energy is required to hit the long ones. Every golfer has experienced hitting long and true shots with swings that felt surprisingly "easy" and "effortless." It is a mystery to them how such "effortless" swings can result in such long shots. To understand how such "effortless" swings can generate such long shots will require some knowledge of the efficient swing. First, it should be obvious that efficiency cannot be attained without the Inside-to-Outside or the Inside-to-Outside-to-Straight clubhead swing path. Secondly, the ball has to be consistently hit on or near the sweet spot of the clubface with swings that are controlled instead of wild. Thirdly, the clubface needs to be relatively square at the moment of impact to impart the greatest energy from the clubhead to the ball. Finally, sufficient clubhead speed is needed.

How much clubhead speed is needed to hit the long ones in an efficient and seemingly "effortless" swing? To answer this question, some simple formulas will be described to give a feeling of the relatively modest amount of energy required to hit long ones with an efficient swing. The formula is that the energy needed is *the energy to swing the clubhead to one third (1/3) the distance of the ball is to travel* for the driver. For those who are curious, our golfing formula can simply be expressed as e =d/3. It means the effort to swing the clubhead is equal to the distance of the ball divided by 3. The remainder of the chapter will explain what this subtle, but extremely potent formula means. In science, a formula can appear to be very simple like $e=mc^2$, which is the formula for producing atomic energy, but it can have extremely potent effect in real life. In this regard, any potent formula needs to be applied with caution, and with safety procedures in mind. Certain safety considerations will be included in the following discussions, and in the section near the end of this chapter. These safety considerations should be taken seriously, and they are not to be ignored.

B. Brief Overview on How the Distance Formulas Work

Energy needed to hit a long shot is the energy needed to swing the clubhead to one third of the ball distance.

According to the above formula, to hit the ball 210 yards with a long iron, for example, the champions swing the clubhead with the energy to send the clubhead (not the ball) to an imaginary distance of 70 yards, which is 1/3 of 210 yards.

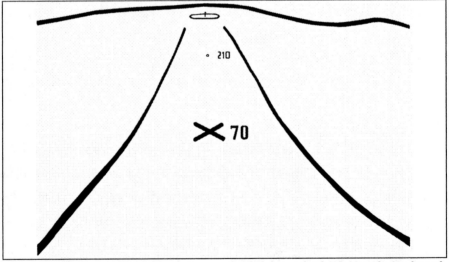

Figure 4-1. Imaginary Distance of Clubhead at 70 Yards Instead of at 210 Yards

To hit the ball 240 yards, the champions swing the clubhead with about 80 yards of energy (240 divided by 3 is 80).

To hit the ball 255 yards, the champions swing the clubhead with about 85 yards of energy (255 divided by 3 is 85).

To drive the ball 270 yards, the champions swing the clubhead with about 90 yards of energy.

To drive the ball 300 yards, the champions swing the clubhead with about 100 yards of energy.

The clubhead is imagined to be swung to a distance that is three times closer than the distance the ball is to be hit to. For example, in Figure 4-1 above, the clubhead is imagined to be swung to the spot marked with an "X" at 70 yards, in order to drive the ball to the spot marked "210" yards. In other words, three times less effort is necessary to swing the clubhead than the distance the ball is to go.

In Figure 4-1, the spot marked with an "X" at

70 yards appears a lot closer than the spot at 210 yards. According to the formula, the clubhead needs to be swung (in an imaginary manner as will be described in the next section in this chapter) to the much closer X-spot at 70 yards instead of the much farther spot at 210 yards. The focus of the swing is shifted to the much closer X-spot.

If the above figure represents a 210 yards par-3 hole, it may feel a very long ways to hit the ball to the hole with a long iron. The hole at 210 yards looks a long ways off. Using the formula, it is not necessary to be concerned with the hole at 210 yards. Only the much closer spot "X" at 70 yards needs to be looked at. All of a sudden, things look and feel shorter and much easier. 70 yards feel a lot more manageable than 210 yards. Champions like Nicklaus described picking an imaginary spot not far in front of the tee to which they use as a focus to swing the clubhead. They forget about the actual far away hole during the swing. Instead, they focus on a spot nearer the tee than the far away hole to swing. This focusing on a nearer spot down the fairway instead of the more distance spot where the ball is to go implies that they have been subconsciously using some variation of the above formulas. Imagining swinging the clubhead to a spot at a distance of 70 yards, and the ball will automatically go to approximately 210 yards.

The formulas, in addition, show the obvious fact that greater energies are needed to swing the clubhead to achieve greater ball distances. Experiences of champions have shown that the increased energies needed to achieve champion level distances increase the risk of injuries, especially as the champions get older. Even though the above formulas contain no limits in term of human endurance, it should be obvious that there are limits to the physical capabilities of champions as well as of any other golfers. While the risk of injuries exists in making shots of any distance, excepting perhaps making putts and short chips, the risk of injuries becomes significantly greater when making extra long shots that the champions need to make. Sam Snead, the long hitting champion, contended that no more than 85 percent of an individual's available power ought to be used during the swing. Some additional safety considerations will be detailed in Section E of this chapter.

The above discussion concludes an overview of how the distance formula works to provide seemingly effortless long shots. A more detailed explanation on how the formula works is presented below.

C. Detailed Explanation of the Distance Formulas

In the slow-motion-picture sequences, the change in clubhead positions during the downswing can be measured from frame to frame and the clubhead speed calculated. In most golfing literature, the energy of the clubhead is expressed as its speed in miles per hour. For example, the long hitting pros can attain a clubhead speed of 120 miles per hour with the driver. Another example is that the average golfer swings the driver clubhead to 90 miles per hour by the time of impact. However, this is an artificial and unnatural way of describing the energy of the speeding clubhead. Humans are not very precise in feeling speed. We only have an approximate feeling of speed as slow, fast, or very fast. There is no way for a human to precisely feel whether the clubhead is traveling at 90 miles per hour or at 100 miles per hour. Both feel fast. The 10 miles per hour difference cannot be felt. That is why car manufacturers install speedometers into cars, as people cannot judge speed very precisely.

It is more natural to describe the energy of the speeding clubhead in terms of distance rather than speed. This may sound very strange at first, but it will make a lot of sense. Take basketball, for instance. People do not describe basketball shots in terms of the speed of the basketball in a shot: for instance, he is making a 25 miles per hour shot. The basketball shot is described as, for example, making a 15 feet shot. Basketball shots are described in terms of distance. He is making a 23-feet shot from the three-point line. He is making a soft 5-feet shot near the basket. Every person who has played basketball understands the meaning, the feel, and the force involved in making a 5-feet shot, a 10-feet shot, a 15-feet shot, a 20-feet shot, and so forth. If the shots are described in terms of ball speed instead of shot distance, no one can comprehend them. No one knows what a 10 miles per hour shot, a 15 miles per hour shot, or a 30 miles per hour shot means nor what it feels like. The miles per hour description may have scientific meaning, but it has no meaning in terms of feel for the players.

Similarly, the energy of the clubhead is commonly described in terms of its speed, in miles per hour, in common literature, which provides very little meaning in terms of feel for the golfers. To be meaningful and to provide feel, the energy of the moving clubhead should be described in terms of the imaginary distance it would have traveled.

Longtime golfers may on rare occasions see, on the golf course or on the driving range, some players swinging with very old drivers, and the clubheads detach from the shaft during the downswing. After detaching from the bottom end of the club's shaft at the bottom of the downswing at impact, the detached clubhead can sail out low to the ground and roll toward the target for around 50 yards. Of course, anytime the clubhead detaches from the shaft creates a dangerous situation, as the loose clubhead can hit and injure someone including the golfer who is swinging the club. The golf club must never be allowed to slip from the hands. Clubheads should be checked for any looseness, and repaired.

However, for this discussion of clubhead energy, the clubhead can be imagined to fly out low to the ground and to continue rolling down the fairway as in the above situation of an old, detached clubhead. The clubhead does not actually fly out. It is only imagined in the mind to fly out. This sort of mental imagining of clubhead flight is used by some of the greatest champions. Nicklaus said that he formed a mental picture of the clubhead swinging through the ball instead of just at the ball. Byron Nelson said that he used a mental picture of the clubhead flying past the ball and beyond. Nelson described that he programmed an image in his mind of the clubhead being "thrown" toward the hole. He did not actually throw the clubhead toward the hole. It was only a feeling in the mind of throwing the clubhead out toward the hole.

While no one can precisely determine clubhead speed in terms of miles per hour, the speed of the clubhead can approximately be felt in terms of the imaginary distance it would have traveled if imagined to detach from the shaft. A slow swing may feel like the clubhead would have traveled 10 imaginary yards. A medium swing may feel like it could have traveled 25 imaginary yards. It is natural, like telling someone to toss a baseball underhanded exactly 12 feet, even as an imaginary toss. It is very unnatural to tell someone to toss the same baseball exactly at 12 miles per hour.

Clubhead energy in terms of distance rather than speed can be summarized in the following three approximate formulas:

Formula #1: For drivers, fairway woods, and long irons: the clubhead imaginary distance is 1/3 (one third) the actual distance of the ball.

Formula #2: For midirons: the clubhead imaginary distance is 1/2 (one half) the distance of the ball.

Formula #3: For short irons: the clubhead imaginary distance is approximately equal to the distance of the ball.

For midirons, the ball flies higher and more energy is expended to make the ball fly up instead of forward. For a 150 yard 5-iron shot to the green, the clubhead needs to be swung with an energy as if to send the clubhead half the way to the green.

For the drivers and long clubs, the ball flies lower. For such a shot, the clubhead needs only to be swung with the energy equal to an imaginary distance 3 times less than the distance the ball is to go. For example, to hit a long iron 180 yards to the flag, the clubhead only needs to be swung with the force to send the clubhead (in the imagination) 60 yards out. Swinging the clubhead to 60 yards feels a lot easier than swinging it to 180 yards. In this example, the long iron needs to be swung with less energy than for a midiron to a shorter distance of 150 yards. A clubhead imaginary distance of 60 yards for the long iron is needed versus a greater clubhead imaginary distance of 75 yards for the midiron according to the formulas. The long iron can be an easier shot than the midirons according to the formulas. While traditionally, the long irons are considered the hardest clubs to use, the formulas may make long irons the easiest clubs to play.

Three times less certainly makes things easier. This goes a long way in explaining why the champions can drive the ball a long way and still maintain balance. It explains why long shots can be produced by what are felt to be "effortless" swings.

The next section of the chapter provides a simplified explanation of how the following formula is derived without going into scientific formulas. A discussion of some safety considerations then follows.

D. How the Distance Formulas are Derived

The ball will go approximately 3 times the imaginary distance of the clubhead.

From laboratory measurements, it is found that the ball picks up about 1.6 times the speed of the clubhead after impact. The ball flies off at a greater speed than the speed of the clubhead, because the ball is lighter than the clubhead.

Many years ago, it was found that the dimples on the ball make the ball fly much further. It was found that even a mighty swing that can fly a dimpled ball 260 yards could hardly fly a ball without any dimples 150 yards. The dimples on the golf ball with backspin enable the ball to glide through the air, as if it had wings, for more distance. The dimples enable the ball to fly about 1.75 times farther.

The total gain for the ball thus far is 1.6 times 1.75 to give 2.8 times as compared to the clubhead. Thus, if the energy of the clubhead makes it go 70 imaginary yards, the ball will go 2.8 times farther: 70 yards times 2.8 gives 196 yards. Assuming an extra 14 yards of roll upon landing, the ball will travel a total of 210 yards (196 + 14 = 210.) Thus, the ball goes approximately 3 times the imaginary distance of the clubhead.

The formula can be written simply as d=3D, where d represents the final distance of the ball, and where D represents the distance of the imaginary clubhead. This amplification of the ball distance by the clubhead can be called the "3D Effect" of golf.

In another words, the clubhead needs to be swung to an imaginary point one third (1/3) the distance of the ball.

To drive the ball 210 yards, the clubhead imaginary distance is 70 yards (3 x 70 = 210). To drive the ball 240 yards, the clubhead imaginary distance is 80 yards (3 x 80 = 240). To drive the ball 270 yards, the clubhead imaginary distance is 90 yards (3 x 90 = 270). To drive the ball 300 yards, the clubhead imaginary distance is 100 yards (3 x100 = 300).

For midirons such as the 5-iron, the ball goes about 2 times instead of 3 times as far, because more energy is used to hit the ball higher. To hit the midiron, the clubhead imaginary distance is about midway to the target.

For short irons, such as the wedge, the ball goes about the same distance as the clubhead imaginary distance. To hit the short irons, the clubhead imaginary distance is all of the way to the target.

The above set of distances of 210, 240, 270 and 300 yards coincide with the average driving distances of average golfers, of advanced amateurs, of touring pros, and of the exceptionally long hitting pros respectively. The average driving distance for the average golfer is actually 200 yards rather than 210 yards in golfing literature. The average driving distance for the touring pros was 250 yards a few decades ago. Now the average has increased to 270 yards for the touring pros. Besides having better clubs and new distance producing golf balls, the modern touring pros are bigger and taller than before. Most of the top champions in the past are just under six feet tall. Today's champions are well over six feet tall.

E. Some Safety Considerations

Although the above set of formulas list shot distances from 210 to 300 yards of the champions, they do not imply that the long distances of the champions should be attempted by just anyone, as there are risks of injuries for those unsuited and unprepared for these great distances. It is like the speedometer in a car. Just because the gauge of the speedometer of a car lists a maximum speed of 160mph, for example, it does not mean the car, especially an older car, can be safely driven to that speed without injury to the car and to the driver. Even a new car may not be equipped by the factory with high-speed tires to withstand the maximum speed indicated on the gauge. Even with the proper tires, they may not be properly inflated. With age, the tires can weaken from wear and tear. They can become out of balance. It becomes unsafe to use them at a speed that they can handle when new. Unless the drivers attend professional training courses for racing, they will for certain make some mistakes at very high speeds that can result in accidents and injuries.

In an analogous way, attempts to swing at champions' distances can cause injuries. Even champions frequently sustain injuries, especially as they get older. They come down with back problems, wrist injuries, tendonitis, hip and other problems. Harmful effects of improper and unsuitable techniques are amplified when swinging for great distances. Slow-motion pictures show that every champion swings with his own unique style, which is natural for his build. No champions swing exactly alike, as they have different builds. Not every champion swings perfectly on an Inside-to-Outside clubhead swing path. Many champions hit fades, which are small slice shots. Some even hit outright slices, although not wild slices. Injuries can result from adopting swing styles that are unnatural or unsuitable for the individual, even if the style is an accepted style, such as the Inside-to-Outside swing. Anything that feels unnatural and which causes strain and pain must be avoided immediately to prevent injuries.

Wear and tear of the body, and the risk of injuries are unavoidable in golf, but they can be minimized. Champions are forced to hit long shots, as holes are made longer in tournament play. The championship tees are moved farther and farther back through the years. Even so, realities have to be taken into account, as senior tour competitions are played from shorter tees. Any pain and injury must be taken cared of immediately by medical doctors before they develop into serious and chronic problems. Medical doctors must be consulted to evaluate the reason for any pain and problems. Teaching golf pros need to be consulted to check for equipment and swing faults, which can cause pain and injuries. For example, intermittent pain in the left palm may mean the development of tendonitis of the left hand due to inappropriate grip size, or excessive grip pressure. A golfer may not understand the seriousness of this condition unless he consults with a doctor. The teaching golf pro can evaluate the grip and the clubs to see if improper swing techniques, and if the equipment are contributing problems. Delays in these check ups can result in problems progressing into serious and chronic injuries. No one should try to be one's own doctor.

Sam Snead advocated that no more than 85 percent of one's available power ought to be used in the golf swing. He promoted swinging within oneself. He said to swing easier, but not overly easy. In this regard, the formulas presented in this book allow the distances to be easily adjusted downward without losing the timing of the swing, for example, by shifting the X-spot from 70 yards to a closer 60 yards, or down to any other shorter distances.

While swinging for too much distance which is inappropriate to the physical ability and to the age of the golfer can be dangerous, developing sufficient distance and accuracy within one's means can literally be life saving in some cases. It is known that some golfers who slice too much and who are unable to have enough distance on long holes have suffered heart attacks while they struggled up from one trouble spot to another among the trees, deep rough and sand traps lining the sides of these long holes.

It is not the intention of this book to address all of the potential injuries that can result from the golf swing. Nor is it claimed that there is sufficient expertise here to treat this subject adequately. The human body is very complex. There are unexpected problems that can potentially occur. For example, if a golfer has a family history of detached retina, will excessive straining in swinging the club to gain inappropriate distances cause this condition to occur? In another example, some champions in the past have been asked whether they breathed in or out during the swing. Could the high rotation speeds of the upper body of some long-hitters cause excess pressure in their chests? Some problems such as spinal disk deterioration, and thinning of bone density can occur without obvious symptoms in the early stages. Timely, and periodic checkups by medical physicians with respect to golfing activities are obviously beneficial, and they are the prudent thing to do in order to avoid serious and chronic injuries.

F. Conclusion

The distance formulas quantify the energy needed to hit shots to given distances. The formulas provide a fairly precise feel of the clubhead speed by using the more intuitive clubhead imaginary distance as the measure. Although not absolutely precise, the formulas provide a fairly accurate picture of how the champions are able to hit such long shots, and still maintain perfect balance throughout the swing that seems effortless.

Appendix

Appendix A

The Slice

When a predominance of side spin over backspin is imparted to the ball, the ball will curve sideways during its flight. Curved ball flight usually occurs when hitting clubs that do not have great loft, as is the case for drivers, fairway woods, the long irons, and even the midirons, such as the 5-iron. The short irons, the sand wedge through the 7-iron, impart so much more backspin over side spin on the ball that shots with the short irons will not have much curvature under normal circumstances. The great amount of backspin tends to keep the flight of the ball straight but not necessarily in the intended direction.

When clockwise side spin is imparted to the ball, the ball curves high and to the right. This type of shot is called a *slice*.

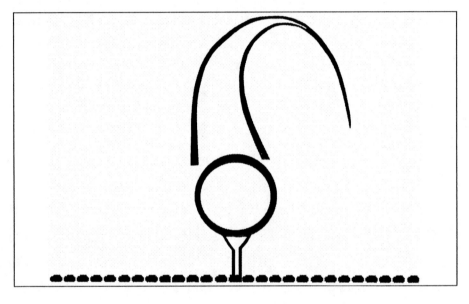

Figure A-1. The Slice

Appendix B

Clubhead Swing Paths

During the downswing, the head of the golf club travels from the high position it takes at the beginning of the downswing down toward the ball. The path the clubhead takes during the downswing is called the *clubhead swing path*. The clubhead can be swung along a great variety of paths to the ball. In order to describe the many paths that the clubhead takes, standard golf terminology has been used to specify these paths.

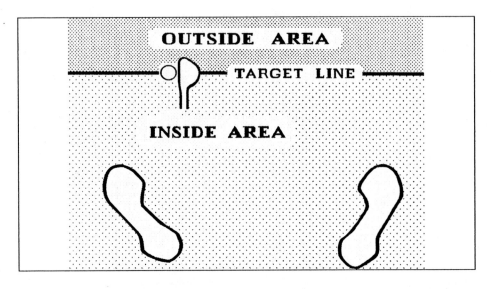

Figure B-1. Inside and Outside Areas

The clubhead swing path during the downswing is the path taken by the center of the clubhead from the beginning of the downswing to the moment the clubhead hits the ball. The *target line* is the imaginary straight line drawn from the ball to the target. The target line further extends to the line behind the ball. The *Inside Area* is the area from the target line back to the area in which the golfer is standing. The inside area also covers the area behind the golfer. The *Outside Area* is the area from the target line to the area away from the golfer as shown in the above diagram. The inside and outside areas are usually just called *inside* and *outside* in golfing parlance.

When the clubhead is said to be traveling on an inside path, it is meant that the center of the clubhead is moving somewhere in the Inside Area, which is on the golfer's side of the target line.

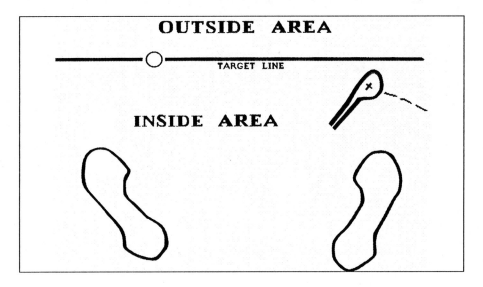

Figure B-2. Clubhead Traveling in the Inside Area

In the above figure, the clubhead is traveling in the area labeled Inside Area, which is below the Target Line in the picture.

When the clubhead is said to be traveling on an outside path, it is meant that the center of the clubhead is moving somewhere in the Outside Area, which is the area on the far side of the target line and in which the golfer is not standing.

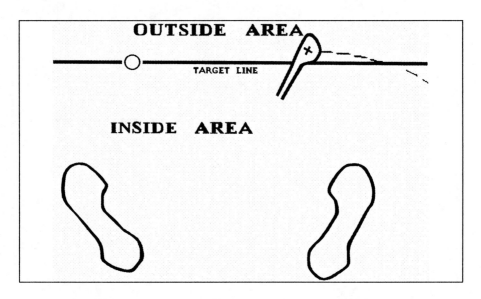

Figure B-3. Clubhead Traveling in the Outside Area

In the Figure B-3, the center of the clubhead as marked by the "+" symbol has crossed above the target line. The center of the clubhead has swung into the outside area before it reaches the ball.

There are, in all, five conceivable paths on

which the clubhead can travel just before hitting the ball:

(a) The clubhead can travel exactly along the target line in a totally straight path to the ball.

(b) The clubhead can travel from an inside to an outside swing path.

(c) The clubhead can travel from an outside to an inside swing path.

(d) The clubhead can travel from an inside to an outside, and then to a straight path.

(e) The clubhead can travel on a path that completely misses the ball.

(a) Clubhead traveling a completely straight path to the ball

The completely straight path into the ball occurs only when the clubhead makes a small back and forth motion in hitting the ball. This only occurs when putting or chipping the ball a short distance. On any full swing, it would be very awkward and impracticable to swing the clubhead in a straight path back and forth.

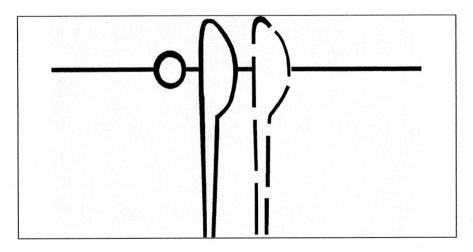

Figure B-4. Totally Straight Path

(b) Clubhead Traveling from an Inside-to-Outside Swing Path Just Before Hitting Ball

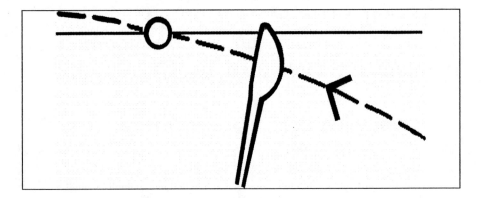

Figure B-5. Inside-to-Outside Path

This is considered by golf pros to be the most acceptable path for the clubhead to travel just before hitting the ball for full shots. The Inside-to-Outside swing path is generally called the *inside-to-out swing path*. Assuming the clubface is fairly square to the target at the moment of impact, an inside-to-out swing path produces draws and hooks, thus eliminating slicing problems.

(c) Clubhead Traveling from an Outside-to-Inside Swing Path Just Before Impact

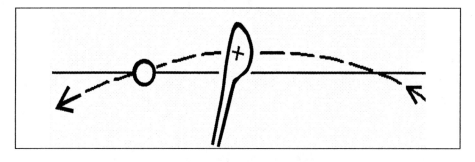

Figure B-6. Outside-to-Inside Path

The clubhead starts in the Inside Area at the beginning of the downswing, but then it is swung out into the Outside Area before reaching the ball. The clubhead is then pulled back toward the Inside Area to hit the ball. The term outside-to-inside refers to the last portion of the clubhead swing path just prior to hitting the ball. The Outside-to-Inside clubhead swing path is the primary—and may be the only—reason for slicing. When the clubhead is swung to the Outside Area early in the downswing, the clubhead must be pulled back toward the Inside Area in order to hit the ball; otherwise, the clubhead will completely miss the ball. When the clubhead is pulled back toward the golfer as the ball is hit, the ball is hit with a cutting action. A slice is produced. Not only will the ball curve to the right during its flight, but a great deal of distance will be lost as the ball will fly higher than intended and land softer. The Outside-to-Inside swing path can also result in the pulled shot, and in the duck hook shot if the clubface is somewhat closed or severely closed at the moment of impact instead of the clubface being squared at impact.

(d) Clubhead Traveling from an Inside-to-Outside-to-Straight Swing Path

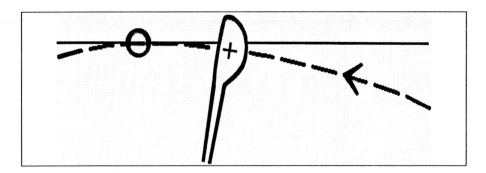

Figure B-7. Inside-to-Outside-to-Straight Path

This clubhead path is similar to the inside-to-out swing path, except that the clubhead path straightens out a little just before the ball is hit, and then swings back to the Inside Area soon after. The center of the clubhead does not ever pass into the outside area.

(e) Clubhead Traveling on a Swing Path That Misses Completely

The paths for complete misses will not be shown as there are too many ways to miss the ball.

This concludes the Appendixes of the book.

Printed in the United States
50537LVS00003B/130